T0365345

Kindergarten and Me

This Is a Preschool Workbook

Paula Warner

ISBN: Softcover   978-1-5434-8473-1
         EBook   978-1-5434-8474-8

Print information available on the last page.

Rev. date: 04/02/2020

To order additional copies of this book, contact:
Xlibris
1-888-795-4274
www.Xlibris.com
Orders@Xlibris.com

I am Little Man, and this baby bear
is one of my favorite toys.

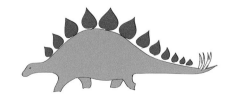

Some people tell me I look like my dad.

In the morning, I eat breakfast, brush
my teeth, and get dressed.

My mother says it is good for me to dress myself. I zip and button my clothes. When I go outside to play, I zip my jacket.

Can you zip a jacket?
Can you button your clothes?

My mother encourages me to tie my own shoes.

Can you tie your sneakers?

I zip my clothes. Zipping is fun.

Jackets   Pants

Coats   Sweaters

Shirts   Zip

Zip

Zip

I even have some shoes that zip.
What can you zip?

I am learning to recognize right and left.

The polar bear and penguin are behind me on your *left* side and my *right* side. The deer and elf is behind me on your *right* side and my *left* side.

I am *outside* playing with my bike.

I am *sitting* on the chair.

Can you find me?

I am standing *adjacent* to the birdbath. My sister is on the *other side* of the birdbath.

I am standing *behind* the dog.

My mother likes pictures of my hands and feet

Hands

Feet

Can you draw a picture of your
hands and feet on this page?

I live at 1616 Mocking Bird Lane in Westbury, Ohio.

Where do you live?_____
_____

My telephone is (254) 915-8300. What is your telephone number? _____
_____

On my head, I have a pair of eyes, ears, some teeth, hair, eyebrows, a nose, and a mouth.

Can you find my ears, eyes, teeth, hair, eyebrows, nose and mouth?

At home, I unpack the car when we go shopping. Another thing I do is practice drawing pictures and playing games with my mother and sister. Mother and I have fun playing "Where are my elbows, eyes, knees, and nose?" game. She tries to grab my nose every time we play.

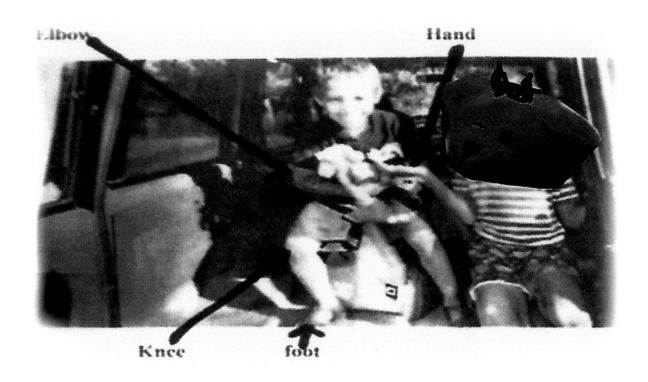

How many *colors* do you recognize?

white *red* *yellow* *blue* *orange* *Pink* *green*

purple

black

Jelly beans

Coloring is fun. My mother says I should practice coloring within the lines.

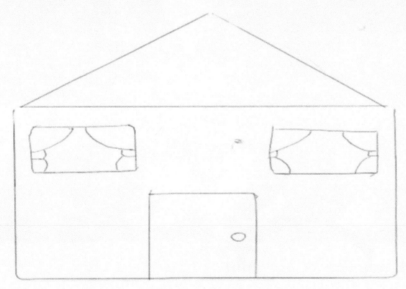

Can you color within the lines?

My sister taught me the alphabet song and how to recognize the letters.

A, B, C, D, E, F, G, H, I, J, K, L, M, N, O, P . . . Q, R, S . . . T, U, V . . . W, X . . . Y and Z.

Now I know my ABCs. Next time won't you sing it with me?

Big A, little a.   Ant begins with a.

Big B, little b·   Basketball begins with b.

Big C, little c.   Clock begins with c.

Big D, little d.   Dog begins with d.

Big E, little e.   Ear begins with e.

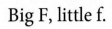 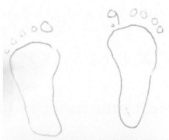

Big F, little f.   Feet begin with f.

Big G, little g.   Grasshopper begins with g.

Big H, little h.   House begins with h.

Big I, little i.   Indian begins with i.

Big J, little J.   Jelly beans begins with j.

Big K, little k.   Kitchen begins with k.

Big L, little l.  Lion begins with l.

Big M, little m.  Mouse begins with m.

Big N, little n.  Nut begin with n.

Big P, little p.  Pool begins with p.

Big Q, little q. Quarter begins with q.

Big R, little r.  Rabbit begins r.

Big S, little s.  Santa begins with s.

Big T, little t.

Telephone begin with t.

Big U, little u.

Umbrella begins with u.

Big V, little v.

Vase begins with v.

Big W, little w.

Welcome begins w.

Big X, little x.

Xylophone begins x.

Big Y, little y.

Yard begins with y.

Big Z, little z.

Zipper begins with z.

Capital letters

A B C D E F G H I J K L M N O P Q R S T U V W X Y Z

A_____
A_____
A_____
A_____
A_____

Small letters

a b c d e f g h i j k l m n o p q r s t u v w x y z

a_____
a_____
a_____
a_____
a_____

Numbers

1 2 3 4 5 6 7 8 9 10 11 12 13 14 15 16 17 18 19 20 21
1_____
1_____
1_____
1_____
1_____
1_____
1_____
1_____

Can you recognize shapes?

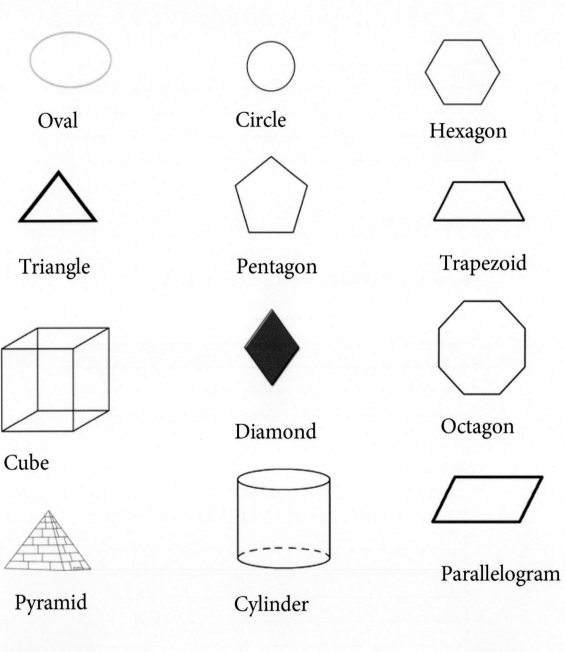

Oval

Circle

Hexagon

Triangle

Pentagon

Trapezoid

Cube

Diamond

Octagon

Pyramid

Cylinder

Parallelogram

Square

Heart

When I started kindergarten, I did not want to leave my baby bear at home. My mother told me I would have fun making new friends at school and that it would not be a good place for my bear. My bear wanted to make friends at school too. Mother brought my baby bear home. It was not a school for bears.

In school, we practice writing our letters. I make large letters and small letters.

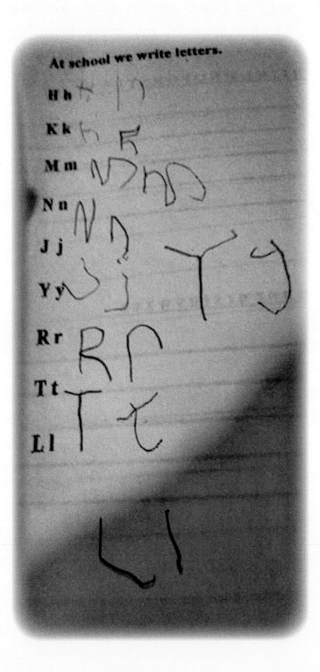

You can practice writing your alphabet here on this page.

Capital Letters

A B C D E F G H I J K L M N O P Q R S T U V W X Y Z

_____

_____

_____

_____

_____

Small Letters

a b c d e f g h i j k l m n o p q r s t u v w x y z

_____

_____

_____

_____

_____

I first learned to count to 10 with my mother. In school we count to 100, by 5's and 10's.

1 2 3 4 5 6 7 8 9 10

Can you write these numbers?

_____

Now let's count by 5's until we reach the number 100.

5 10 15 20 25 30 35 40 45 50 55 60 65 70 75 80 85 90 95 100

Can you write these numbers too?

_____

_____

Try counting to one hundred one number at a time.

1 ___	20 ___	39 ___	58 ___	77 ___	96 ___
2 ___	21 ___	40 ___	59 ___	78 ___	97 ___
3 ___	22 ___	41 ___	60 ___	79 ___	98 ___
4 ___	23 ___	42 ___	61 ___	80 ___	99 ___
5 ___	24 ___	43 ___	62 ___	81 ___	100 ___
6 ___	25 ___	44 ___	63 ___	82 ___	
7 ___	26 ___	45 ___	64 ___	83 ___	
8 ___	27 ___	46 ___	65 ___	84 ___	
9 ___	28 ___	47 ___	66 ___	85 ___	
10 ___	29 ___	48 ___	67 ___	86 ___	
11 ___	30 ___	49 ___	68 ___	87 ___	
12 ___	31 ___	50 ___	69 ___	88 ___	
13 ___	32 ___	51 ___	70 ___	89 ___	
14 ___	33 ___	52 ___	71 ___	90 ___	
15 ___	34 ___	53 ___	72 ___	91 ___	
16 ___	35 ___	54 ___	73 ___	92 ___	
17 ___	36 ___	55 ___	74 ___	93 ___	
18 ___	37 ___	56 ___	75 ___	94 ___	
19 ___	38 ___	57 ___	76 ___	95 ___	

In school, we talk about the days of the week and the twelve months of the year. My class sings the "days of the week" song. These are the words to the song.

Sunday, Monday . . . Tuesday, Wednesday . . . Thursday, Friday, Saturday.
Sunday, Monday . . . Tuesday, Wednesday . . . Thursday, Friday, Saturday . . . the days of the week.

These are some of the things I do during the week.

Sunday is the first day of the week. I meet my church family at the building on Sunday.

Monday is the second day of the week but it is the first day of school.

Tuesday is the second day of school and a day when I get ready for a test.

Wednesday is the middle of the week and a day we have fun and play together.

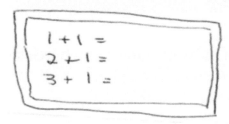

Thursday is test day at school.

Friday is the last day of school for the work week and we are happy.

Saturday is a relaxing day for me and my bear. We sleep late on Saturday.
Where do you go during the week?

My school teacher talks about the signs of the seasons. We do not go to school during the summer. My favorite season is fall.

Fall

Summer

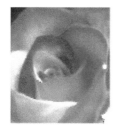  

Winter

Spring

Matching is looking for twins or things that look alike. On my test, I got all matching questions correct.

Can you match these items?

In school, we learn about places such as *under, on, behind,* and *inside.*
My first school trip was to Old McDonald's farm. After the trip, I fell asleep *on* the bus with my head *on* a bag of apples. The apples are *under* my head.

During a family trip to the museum, we took pictures. This picture shows me standing in *front* of a dinosaur. The dinosaur is standing *behind* me. I like dinosaurs. I play with toy dinosaurs at home.

I am sitting *inside* the doorway of the playhouse at school.

It's just me sitting *on* the floor.

Do you know what time it is?

What time do you get up?_____

What time do you eat breakfast?_____

What time do you eat lunch?_____

What time do you eat dinner?_____

What time do you go to bed?_____

What time is it now?_____

My bear watches learn to read and write.

School will end soon and I will have some summer fun. My mother says I should continue practicing writing and learning to read so I can be ready for the next school year.

Printed in the United States
By Bookmasters